Contents

Foreword

Reading the European Convention on Human Rights fifty years after it was written, you are struck by the fact that children barely feature in it at all. It is by the application and renovation of the principles it sets out that children have come to be accorded at least some of the protections it accords to adults. The first social right to feature in the Convention is the right to education; but it remains a right heavily qualified by considerations of availability. There is no separate recognition of a child's right to security or, within its natural limits, autonomy: these have had to be deduced from the provisions for security of person and respect for private and family life, and in neither case do they sit comfortably with the adult-oriented drafting of the Convention. One of the accepted tasks of the European Court of Human Rights, and now of our own courts, is to continue the process of bridging this gap in what is universally recognised as a living instrument, not a dry text.

For us in the United Kingdom there is a particular concern, as the Human Rights Act brings the Convention into effect here, about the possible impact of Article 8 upon the paramountcy of the child's interests established by Section 1 of the Children Act 1989. Is an abusive parent going to be allowed to cut down that fundamental protection by invoking the right to respect for his or her family life? Or will the primacy of the child's welfare be seen as the fundamental object of all family life, and Section 1 be upheld intact?

Even when this is resolved, much will remain undecided. Will children continue to be hit when to do the same to an adult would be a crime? Can the measures available in law for the safety or containment of children be fitted within the Article 5 exceptions? Behind all such questions lies the constitutional shift we are undergoing from liberties to rights. From it will flow a need to reconsider how our ideas about personal autonomy and adult authority fit with the entitlements of children to respect and protection.

These ought not to be questions for lawyers and childcare professionals only. They are questions that every parent, every teacher and every growing child should be able to understand and think about. They need to be a site not of confrontation but of discussion and negotiation. So a booklet like this one, written in straightforward prose for ordinary people of all ages, is a real contribution to a process vital to our democracy. The process of giving living and worthwhile effect to human rights in the interests of those citizens who are always seen but in truth rarely heard – children.

Rt Hon Lord Justice Sedley
Royal Courts of Justice

Acknowledgements

Many people contributed to the making of this booklet. Thanks to Kieran Breen, Nicola Chapman and others at Save the Children for their work. Thanks to all those who commented on drafts, in particular Allan Levy QC, Rowena Daw, Cath Casserley, Veena Vasista and Deborah King. Thanks to Stephen Sedley LJ, for agreeing to write the foreword.

This is dedicated to my parents Rani and John Drew and to my sister Anita and brother Jonathan Iqbal Drew: all unique, all beloved.

Abbreviations

ECHR – European Convention on Human Rights

HRA – Human Rights Act 1998

UN Convention on the Rights of the Child – United Nations Convention on the Rights of the Child

ILO – International Labour Organisation

Introduction

This booklet aims to introduce people and organisations working with children to the use of the Human Rights Act 1998 in the advocacy of children's rights. Laws set standards, and we intend this information to be used for education and negotiation as much as for litigation. Where legal action is necessary, this booklet is intended as an introduction rather than as a detailed guide. At the back of the booklet there is information on where to get advice and support.

In this booklet, children are taken to be people under eighteen. All children have rights. However, though it is hoped to encourage a general culture favourable to children's rights, this booklet focuses on the particular problems faced by the children with whom Save the Children is concerned:

- children disadvantaged by poverty, discrimination and exclusion

- children with special needs

- children without families or in care

- refugee children.

What is the Human Rights Act 1998?

The Human Rights Act 1998 has been passed to give further effect to certain rights. It is intended as a first step towards a full Bill of Rights.

The rights to which the Act gives further effect already exist in the European Convention of Human Rights (see below), but the Act will make it much easier to raise these rights within the UK. It states that a public authority shall not act in a way which is incompatible with the rights set out. The Act is already in force in Scotland and Wales, and came into force in England and Northern Ireland on 2 October 2000.

What is the European Convention on Human Rights?

Hereafter referred to as the ECHR, it is a regional human rights instrument drawn up by the member states of the Council of Europe in 1950.

The rights agreed are set out in the form of Articles, which can be summarised as follows:

Article 1:   The state shall secure the right

Article 2:   The right to life

Article 3:   Freedom from torture, inhuman or degrading treatment

Article 4:   Freedom from slavery or servitude, forced or compulsory labour

Article 5:   The right not to be unlawfully detained

Article 6:   The right to a fair hearing

Article 7:   Freedom from retrospective penalties

Article 8:   The right to respect for private and family life, for home and correspondence

Article 9:   Freedom of religion, thought and conscience

Article 10: Freedom of expression and freedom to receive information without interference

Article 11: Freedom of association

Article 12: The right to marry

Article 13: The right to an effective remedy

Article 14: The right not to be discriminated against in the enjoyment of these rights.

Articles 1 and 13 are not part of the Human Rights Act 1998, since the UK Government argues that the Act in itself has the aim of securing rights and providing an effective remedy. Articles 7 and 12 do not obviously give rise to issues that affect children. The other Articles will be examined in greater detail in this booklet.

Since 1950 there have been additional agreements, called Protocols to the Convention. Apart from Article 2 of Protocol 1, which sets out a right to education, they will not be examined here.

Individuals are able, and will continue to be able, to take cases raising breaches of their rights to the European Court of Human Rights at Strasbourg once they have exhausted all remedies in the UK.

The rights set out above clearly reflect the immediate post-war concern for civil and political rights (such as freedom of expression or religion) rather than for social and economic rights (for example, the right to food or clean water).

Fundamental rights are expressed in general terms. How they are interpreted will change as society changes. Because of this, the ECHR should be read as a living instrument. Freedom of expression, for example, intended in 1950 to cover the right to express dissenting political opinions, is now just as likely to be interpreted as including the right to express a different sexuality. Even though the drafters of the ECHR probably did not have sexuality in mind, it is in the nature of such fundamental rights that they evolve with society. How these rights, which are the "ground rules" of our society, are interpreted will depend upon the cases identified and brought by children and their advocates.

Another important principle is to read these rights so that they are practical and effective rather than mere paper rights.

Can these rights be interfered with?

Some of the rights (such as freedom from torture) cannot be interfered with in any way. Others (such as the rights contained in Articles 5 and 8 and the freedoms set out in Articles 9, 10 and 11) can be interfered with. The following checklist will help you to decide whether the interference is permitted.

Checklist: Is the interference permitted?

Is it lawful ("according to law"/"prescribed by law")?

Is it predictable?

Is it accessible?

Is the interference pursuant to one of the aims set out in the Article?

If Yes:

Is it necessary in democratic society?

Does it answer a pressing social need?

Are the means proportionate to the aim?

In international law, a state, when agreeing to a right, can reserve the right either to depart from the right completely or to observe the right in a limited way. The position is arguably different where the state has given further effect to the rights in domestic courts. The UK has entered a reservation to part of the right to education, on the basis of efficient teaching and use of resources.

A right should not be read so as to narrow the scope of another right: for example, the right to information cannot be read so as to narrow the scope of the right to a private life.

Will this history and these principles remain relevant?

Yes. In deciding a case under the Act, the court must take into account ECHR case law and principles of interpretation. This does not mean that the courts will have to follow ECHR case law, which should provide a "floor" rather than a "ceiling". Children's advocates may refer to other material, such as constitutional cases from other jurisdictions – for example, the USA, India, Canada, South Africa, New Zealand or Australia – and other human rights conventions and statements of principle.

There is another important difference between cases decided by the European Court of Human Rights in Strasbourg and cases decided by courts in the UK. The Strasbourg court left member states some discretion in implementing the rights, particularly in areas where there was a lack of consensus across Europe. This discretion is likely to disappear when courts in the UK look at cases: the UK courts will not only be less distant from national conditions than the Strasbourg court, but will themselves be under a duty to act so as to make the rights effective. However, some argue that the courts will still leave the executive some discretion where policy decisions are involved and depending on the nature of the right.

What about the UN Convention on the Rights of the Child (1989)?

This is a United Nations instrument, worldwide rather than regional. It was drawn up with child rights specifically in mind, and is much more detailed than the ECHR. The UN Convention on the Rights of the Child has been agreed by every state in the world (except Somalia and the USA) and therefore the principles set out in it can be regarded as generally accepted. In deciding cases before it, the Strasbourg court has referred not only to the Convention itself but to reviews of country reports by the UN Committee on the Rights of the Child (for example, in its reviews of the UK's 1995 Report, the Committee criticised the width of the defence of reasonable chastisement).

The ECHR did not deal specifically with children's rights. However, the Council of Europe has not overlooked the matter. In 1979 there was an unsuccessful proposal for an additional protocol on children's rights. In 1990 Recommendation 1121 advised implementation of the UN Convention on the Rights of the Child as the best way of promoting children's rights in Europe. A 1992 Recommendation has set out a Charter of Children's Rights in Europe. A 1995 European Convention on the Exercise of Children's Rights, setting out the procedural rights of children and the special duties courts are under when hearing cases affecting children, has not yet been signed up to by the UK. Recommendation 1286 of 1996 urged member states to implement the UN Convention on the Rights of the Child by withdrawing any reservations and reviewing and adapting legislative and regulatory provisions. It also referred to the 1995 Convention. In 1998 the Council of Europe launched a Programme for Children.

Although the ECHR, because it was not conceived as a charter for children, makes no reference to the best interests of the child as being primary or paramount in decisions, it is probable that the courts will refer to this principle, since it appears both in the UN Convention on the Rights of the Child and in national legislation such as the Children Act 1989. It is likely that courts will continue to put the interests of the child first in family cases, and the principle may have some effect in health, education, social security and immigration issues.

Who has duties under the Human Rights Act?

Public authorities have a duty not to act incompatibly with the rights. However, this duty is not directly imposed on the private sector or on private individuals. Whether or not a body is public is therefore an important question.

In many cases the answer will be obvious: for example, where a local education authority or a hospital is involved. If a body is not obviously public but carries out functions of a public nature, it will be regarded as a public authority, but only in relation to those public functions.

Checklist: Is it public?

Is it part of a statutory system?

But for the existence of the body, would parliament legislate?

Does the body operate under authority of government?

Is the duty of public significance?

Is there extensive use of monopolistic powers?

Does it affect the rights of individuals in ways going beyond how a private act might affect them?

For example, the security firm Group 4 will be a public authority in respect of detention powers, which are public. So will children's homes in respect of their duties.

The courts will also have duties under the Act. This means that court structures and procedures should be child-friendly. It also means that the courts will have to interpret the law, wherever possible, so as to be compatible with the rights. This is an advance on the traditional practice of the courts, where the ECHR was looked at only in cases of ambiguity. This interpretative duty is likely to affect many cases brought before the courts, including those involving private bodies, and will thus create an indirect effect on private bodies.

What does the duty not to act incompatibly with the rights in the Act mean?

In some cases, the duty on public authorities does not go beyond the duty not to interfere unlawfully with a right. This will include interference by omission as well as by act. In other cases, a public authority has a positive obligation. This means a duty to do something, rather than a duty not to do something. A public authority will therefore also be required to consider the impact on children of omissions as well as acts.

Depending on the particular right, this may include:

- Changing structures, procedures and policies where they breach a right

- Making decisions that give sufficient weight to the right at stake

- Preventing the breach of a right, whether in the public or the private sphere. This may include setting up a system of prevention through effective deterrents

- Remedying a breach of a right

- Providing information that enables individuals to make an informed assessment of their right and any breach

- Providing resources.

It is fundamental to a culture of respect for children's rights that children who are capable of forming their own views should have their voice heard when their own rights are being determined. This means ensuring that decision-making allows the voice of the child to be heard and to be given due weight, whether through consultation, representation or a complaints procedure.

Many decisions have an impact on children, even when the children are not obviously involved directly. In such a case, the child's right should be considered and respected. For example, in July 1998 an appeal to the Indian Supreme Court against a sentence of death included the ground that the court should consider the effect on the appellant's child of her mother's death.

Can legislation be struck down if it is a breach of the Act?

Acts of Parliament, even if they are a breach of a right, cannot be struck down by the courts. This does not include subordinate legislation (such as Regulations) or legislation passed by the Scottish Parliament or the Welsh Assembly. This immunity extends to decisions that are the direct and only possible result of Acts of Parliament.

The courts can, however, declare that a piece of primary legislation is incompatible with the Human Rights Act. It would be expected that, following such a declaration, the government would change the legislation.

When new legislation is introduced, it will be accompanied either by a statement that it is compatible with the rights set out in the Human Rights Act or by a statement that no statement can be made. This will provide an opportunity for children's advocates to point out any incompatibility. Legislation may, of course, still be challenged by bringing an application directly under the ECHR to Strasbourg.

Who has rights under the Human Rights Act?

Everyone in the UK, regardless of citizenship or immigration status, will have rights under the Human Rights Act.

However, anyone bringing a case under the Act must be a "victim": that is, they must show that they at least run the risk of being directly affected. A woman would be able to challenge a prohibition on abortion, even if she were not pregnant. A man would not.

A court may now make an order that a child, if judged sufficiently responsible, may bring or defend claims without a litigation friend. Children who are not responsible enough to bring a claim themselves may appoint someone to act as their litigation friend.

Children's rights organisations can become involved in a number of ways. They may act as a litigation friend. They may provide general support or intervene in proceedings as a "friend of the court" in order to explain the issues involved and give background information. Arguably, they may claim that they too are the victim of a breach if they can show that they are an organisation *of* children as well as *for* children.

Specific rights

The specific rights in the Human Rights Act are described below. Each entry contains a summary of the Article as it may be explained to a child, an explanation of the right conferred by the Article and a list of situations to which the Article might apply. Reference is made to similar rights in the UN Convention on the Rights of the Child.

Because the Act is to be read as a living instrument in the light of present-day conditions, each entry looks at how the Article concerned might be applied to current children's issues. This does not mean that such arguments will automatically succeed, and expert advice should be sought before taking legal action.

Article 2: The right to life

1. Everyone's life shall be protected by law.

2. Deprivation of life shall not be regarded as contravening this article when it results from the use of force that is no more than absolutely necessary:

   a) in defence of any person from unlawful violence;

   b) in order to effect a lawful arrest or to prevent the escape of a person lawfully detained;

   c) in action lawfully taken for the purpose of quelling a riot or insurrection.

☞ **Everyone should recognise that you have the right to live.**

This Article prohibits the state from taking life, except in the situations set out. The death penalty is also provided for in this Article, but by Protocol 6 it has been abolished for peacetime.

Not only is the state under an obligation not to take life, but it must also take steps to safeguard the lives of those within its jurisdiction. This includes preventing one person's life being taken by another. In a recent case involving the failure of a police force to anticipate that a campaign of stalking would end in killing, the European Court held that the question was whether the state knew, or ought to have known, of a real and immediate risk to life, and whether it had failed to take measures that might have been expected to avoid that risk.

This Article applies to medical treatment and to healthcare generally. It is unlikely that the Article will be held to apply to abortions.

The Supreme Court of India, and more recently the South African Constitutional Court, has held that the right to life includes a right to a life worth living: that is to say, physical, mental and social well-being. Unlike the UN Convention on the Rights of the Child, Article 2 does not include a right of children to development. It is arguable, however, that a wide reading of the Article would extend to development, since the European Charter on Children's Rights refers to the right to development. A further argument in favour of a wide interpretation is the basic principle that this right must be interpreted in a way that makes the enjoyment of other rights effective.

Case study

Child B had leukaemia. She sought treatment by way of chemotherapy and a second bone-marrow transplant. Her local health authority refused to fund the treatment.

Child B challenged this decision in the courts. The authority claimed that it was not in the child's best interests to have treatment which would prolong suffering and that the treatment was an ineffective use of resources. Neither reason was found to be satisfactory by the judge in the High Court, who held that where so fundamental a right as life was involved, any decision, whether in the form of an act or an omission, that ended it must be closely scrutinised by the court and had to be justified on substantial public-interest grounds. The judge commented that, although the chance of life offered by the operation was modest, to anyone confronting the prospect of extinction any chance of survival must be unimaginably precious. He also held that where there was even a slim chance of saving the life of a ten-year-old child, the authority had to do more than "toll the bell of slim resources".

The Court of Appeal overturned this decision. It held that it could only assess the lawfulness of the decision. It commented that it was well known that health authorities had limited resources.

The approach of the High Court judge is likely to be more compatible with the Act and the one to be followed both by a health authority and by a court.

Possible issues

The following may give rise to issues under Article 2:

- Decisions about the medical treatment of an ill child

- Other decisions on healthcare: for example, calculations of the value of an operation in cases of reduced life expectancy

- Deportation of children to a risk of death

- Inadequate policies on, and sanctions against, speeding on roads

- The right to life may arise if a hospital seeks court authority to give a Jehovah's Witness who is under eighteen a blood transfusion against his or her wishes. This issue has so far been decided on the basis that the child's consent to die was not an informed consent.

See also: *Human Rights Act 1998:* Article 3
UN Convention on the Rights of the Child: Article 6; Article 24

Article 3: Freedom from torture, inhuman and degrading treatment

No one shall be subjected to torture or to inhuman or degrading treatment or punishment.

☞ **Whether or not you do something wrong, no one should treat you or punish you in a way that frightens you or hurts you badly.**

This Article is likely to be one of the most effective in protecting children's rights.

Treatment must meet a minimum level of severity to be "inhuman or degrading". The threshold of acceptable treatment will vary with the evolving standards of society. Treatment is likely to be inhuman if it causes intense physical or mental suffering. Treatment is likely to be degrading if it arouses feelings of anguish, fear and inferiority capable of humiliating the victim.

Whether treatment is sufficiently serious depends on:

- The nature and context of the treatment

- Its duration

- Its physical and mental effects

- The sex, age and state of health of the victim.

What will determine the matter is the effect of the treatment, not the motive for administering it. In many circumstances, the treatment may have a much more severe effect on children than on adults.

The state has an obligation to take steps to prevent the treatment occurring, as well as an obligation not to torture or degrade the child itself. It will not be sufficient for the state simply to prohibit such treatment. It must ensure a mechanism of protection that extends to physical punishment, provided it is severe enough, of a child in a private school and within the family.

Case study 1

A, a nine-year-old boy, had been severely beaten by his stepfather. In criminal proceedings for assault, the stepfather's defence was lawful chastisement, which in cases of assault on children can be raised only by parents or people acting in the place of parents.

The state was held responsible for providing protection against the severe treatment of a child within the family. The existence and breadth of the defence meant that the law did not offer proper protection. Statistics produced by the government showing that convictions did occur were held to be unreliable since they did not show instances of assaults that were not pursued. A breach of Article 3 was found.

A also argued that as a child he was discriminated against, since the defence would not have been available in a case involving an assault on an adult.

Case study 2

Four children suffered severe ill-treatment or neglect by their parents. They were referred to social services in 1987 by the health visitor, but after meetings were held the file was closed. Subsequently the family was reported to social services by the police, the children's school, the NSPCC, the children's grandmother and respite carers. Meetings and a case conference were held, but no decision was made to go to court.

At one stage the mother asked that two of the children be placed for adoption. She also asked that they be placed in care and said that, if they were not, she would batter them. The children were entered on the Child Protection Register. All four were fostered. Full care orders were made in 1993. The children brought a claim against the local authority, but the UK courts held that the authority did not have a duty of care. The children then went to Strasbourg, where at the first stage the Commission said:

> *The Commission considers that the protection of children who by reason of their age and vulnerability are not capable of protecting themselves requires not merely that the criminal law should provide protection against Article 3 treatment but that, additionally, this provision will in appropriate circumstances imply a positive obligation on the authorities to take preventive measures to protect a child who is at risk from another individual. The Commission notes in this regard the international recognition accorded to this principle in Article 19 of the UN Convention on the Rights of the Child, which enjoins States to take all appropriate measures "to protect the child from all forms of physical and mental violence, injury or abuse".*

> *…The Commission considers that [the local authority] may be regarded as subject to the positive obligation to take those steps that could be reasonably expected of them to avoid a real and immediate risk of ill-treatment contrary to Article 3 of which they knew or ought to have had knowledge.*

The case will now be heard by the Court.

Possible issues

The following may give rise to issues under Article 3:

• Neglect or abuse at home or in care: see, for example, the findings of the *Lost in Care* report produced in 2000 after the Waterhouse Inquiry into the treatment of children in care in Wales between 1974 and 1994 and the criticisms of six local authorities, social workers, the police and the Welsh Office

- Conditions in institutions or in detention, especially for children who are particularly vulnerable to poor conditions, such as those with special needs

- Bullying. This may include bullying by other pupils outside school hours and off school premises if linked to behaviour inside school, since most bullying policies include bullying to and from school, and schools have a responsibility for behaviour by pupils off school premises

- Child refugees and separation from parents

- Trafficking in children

- Conditions of homeless children

- Child-beating at home or in school

- Circumcision

- Discrimination

- The effect of decisions about prisoners on their children: for example, placement in a prison where visits are difficult for the children.

See also: *Human Rights Act 1998:* Article 14
UN Convention on the Rights of the Child: Article 19; Article 37(a); Article 39

Article 4: Freedom from slavery or servitude, forced or compulsory labour

1. No one shall be held in slavery or servitude.

2. No one shall be required to perform forced or compulsory labour.

3. For the purposes of this Article, the term forced or compulsory labour shall not include:

a) any work required to be done in the ordinary course of detention imposed according to the provisions of Article 5 of this Convention or during conditional release after such detention;

b) any service of a military character or, in the case of conscientious objectors in countries where they are recognised, service instead of compulsory military service;

c) any service exacted in the course of an emergency or calamity threatening the life or well-being of the nation;

d) any work or service which forms part of normal civic duties.

☞ **You do not have to work unless you want to.**

There have been very few cases brought in respect of forced or compulsory labour, and even fewer claiming slavery or servitude.

The European Court has stated that the Conventions agreed under the auspices of the International Labour Organisation (ILO) are relevant in looking at this right.

The Article does not forbid child labour in all circumstances. The common characteristic of slavery or servitude or forced or compulsory labour is that the agreement of the worker to work is absent. The fact that the work may be paid does not prevent it from being forced or compulsory. The first question is whether the work is done under the threat of physical force or the threat of a penalty. The second question is whether agreement was real, informed and given freely.

> *What there has to be is work exacted under menace of any penalty and also performed against the will of the person concerned: that is, work for which he has not offered himself voluntarily . . .*
>
> *Prior consent, without more, does not therefore warrant the conclusion that the obligations incumbent on him . . . did not constitute [compulsory labour] if service imposed a burden which was so excessive or disproportionate to the advantages attached . . . that the service could not be treated as having been voluntarily accepted beforehand.*
> (Van der Mussele v Belgium)

Special considerations arise when deciding whether a child has consented to work. Children are in a weaker position to negotiate an employment contract and are more vulnerable to exploitation. Consent to work may also have been obtained under a threat, such as being reported to an immigration or local authority. In such cases it is difficult to see how there could be real agreement.

It is also arguable that where working conditions fall below a certain standard so that the burden of the work is excessive, the conclusion may be that consent was not properly obtained. This might be the case where the work is being done by someone below the minimum age for employment or for below the minimum wage. The Article should also be read as a living instrument in the light of present-day social conditions. Guidance on what is unacceptable employment for children is given by the ILO Worst Forms of Child Labour Convention 1999 (not yet signed up to by the UK). This defines the worst forms of child labour as:

(a) all forms of slavery or practices similar to slavery, such as the sale and trafficking of children, debt bondage and serfdom and forced or compulsory labour, including forced or compulsory recruitment of children for use in armed conflict;

(b) the use, procuring or offering of a child for prostitution, for the production of pornography or for pornographic performances;

(c) the use, procuring or offering of a child for illicit activities, in particular for the production and trafficking of drugs as defined in the relevant international treaties;

(d) work which, by its nature or the circumstances in which it is carried out, is likely to harm the health, safety or morals of children.

The Child Labour Convention covers working conditions which are so poor that the state has a duty to intervene. This must be on the basis that there was no agreement or that conditions were so poor that there can have been no consent. It should be noted, however, that the Child Labour Convention is wider than the terms of Article 4.

The Convention requires immediate and effective measures to secure the prohibition and elimination of the worst forms of child labour. It emphasises the importance of education and social development as a means of eliminating the worst forms of child labour. It stresses the need for the following action:

1. Taking measures to eliminate the worst forms of child labour, including co-ordination of relevant agencies.

2. Promoting education and vocational training.

3. Alleviating poverty and supporting the families of children.

4. Reaching out to children at special risk.

5. Providing rehabilitation and social integration.

6. Taking account of the special situation of girls.

The importance placed on education as a means of eliminating exploitative labour should be noted.

Possible issues

The following may give rise to issues under Article 4:

- Whether or not the police, local authorities, social workers and others have effective and co-ordinated mechanisms for identifying, preventing and eliminating exploitative labour practices

- The extent to which exploitative labour practices in the hidden economy, in the employment of domestic workers and in particular among children subject to immigration control are prevented. Given the emphasis of the ILO Convention, this is likely to include the provision of adequate education and support. It may also include avoiding policies that result in the incurring of excessive debts by families entering the UK

- Courts which might otherwise have been restricted from hearing an employment or personal injury claim because of immigration irregularities or non-payment of taxes on the part of employer or child, or because of diplomatic immunity, may now be able to hear the claim

- Military service is allowed by the Article. However, there is no specific authorisation for the conscription of children, and this is unlikely to be held to be permitted, given the existence of the Optional Protocol to the UN Convention on the Rights of the Child, which imposes eighteen as the minimum age for participation in armed conflict or for conscription. Sixteen is the minimum age under the Protocol for voluntary recruitment, but this may lead to breaches of Article 3 if conditions have a sufficiently severe effect.

See also: *Human Rights Act 1998:* Article 3; Article 6; Article 5
UN Convention on the Rights of the Child: Article 32

Article 5: The right not to be unlawfully detained

1. Everyone has the right to liberty and security of person. No one shall be deprived of his liberty save in the following cases and in accordance with a procedure prescribed by law:

   a) the lawful detention of a person after conviction by a competent court;

b) the lawful arrest and detention of a person for non-compliance with the lawful order of a court or in order to secure the fulfilment of any obligation prescribed by law;

c) the lawful arrest and detention of a person effected for the purpose of bringing him before the competent legal authority on reasonable suspicion of having committed an offence or when it is reasonably considered necessary to prevent his committing an offence or fleeing after having done so;

d) the detention of a minor by lawful order for the purpose of educational supervision or his lawful detention for the purpose of bringing him before the competent legal authority;

e) the lawful detention of persons for the prevention of the spreading of infectious diseases, of persons of unsound mind, alcoholics or drug addicts or vagrants;

f) the lawful arrest or detention of a person to prevent his effecting an unauthorised entry into the country or of a person against whom action is being taken with a view to deportation or extradition.

2. Everyone who is arrested shall be informed promptly, in a language which he understands, of the reasons for his arrest and of any charge against him.

3. Everyone arrested or detained in accordance with the provisions of paragraph 1 (c) of this Article shall be brought promptly before a judge or other officer authorised by law to exercise judicial power and shall be entitled to trial within a reasonable time or to release pending trial. Release shall be conditioned by guarantees to appear for trial.

4. Everyone who is deprived of his liberty by arrest or detention shall be entitled to take proceedings by which the lawfulness of his detention shall be decided speedily by a court and his release ordered if the detention is not lawful.

5. Everyone who has been the victim of arrest or detention in contravention of the provisions of this Article shall have an enforceable right to compensation.

☛ You have the right not to be shut away unless you have done something wrong or unless you need to be shut away to make sure that you learn. Even then, you should be shut away only if it is lawful. If you think you should not be shut away, you have the right to see a judge about this.

Detention may take place only in the situations set out above.

Paragraph 1 (d) specifically refers to the detention of children. The Article does not define educational supervision. Measures taken to deal with children in the juvenile justice system under welfare rather than criminal provisions are likely to fall within the scope of this provision.

Paragraph 1 (e) specifically refers to the detention of "persons of unsound mind". Unlike Paragraph 1 (d), this does not refer to children.

Paragraph 1 (f) refers to detention within the immigration system. Again, there is no specific reference to children.

However, even where the purpose falls within one of the categories set out above, the detention will still be a breach of the Article if it is not carried out according to law. This includes the use of proper procedures and the observation of the principle that detention should be for no longer than necessary.

It also includes the following general legal principles:

- Owing to their special situation, child refugees should not be detained (UN High Commission for Refugees)

- Detention should be a last resort for children and must be for the shortest possible time: see the Rules for the Protection of Juveniles adopted by the UN General Assembly in 1990

- Detained children should be kept separate from adults

- There should be continued access to the child

- The detention should be kept under constant review.

The ECHR has held that the fact that it was a mother who placed her son in a mental hospital did not absolve the state from its duty to be unremittingly vigilant that the detention was lawful.

Possible issues

The following may give rise to issues under Article 5:

- The use of detention centres for children subject to immigration control

- Detention for the purpose of medical treatment when the child's consent has not been sought – even where he or she is competent – or when the child's refusal has been overridden

- Use of Secure Training Orders and Secure Training Centres where community schemes for educational training, operating under supervision orders, have not been explored

- Detention of children with adults

- Detention of juvenile offenders

- Informal admission to psychiatric hospitals

- Detention awaiting trial

- Detention as an alternative to care

- Use of secure accommodation orders

- Detention at Her Majesty's Pleasure

- Place of safety orders

- Removals for adoption or fostering.

Checklist

Does the detention fall within one of the situations described in Article 5?

Has it been carried out according to law?

- Is there a legal provision which appears to authorise the detention?

- Are there any relevant children's provisions which suggest that detention should not be imposed in this case?

- Has the necessity for the detention been regularly reviewed by someone acting in a judicial capacity?

- If a court has authorised the detention of a child, did it do so according to law? Has the child been given a voice in any such proceeding?

- Is there access to a court to review the lawfulness of the detention?

See also: *Human Rights Act 1998*: Article 3; Article 6; Article 14
      UN Convention on the Rights of the Child: Article 37 (detention a last resort)

Article 6: The right to a fair hearing

1. In the determination of his civil rights and obligations or of any criminal charge against him, everyone is entitled to a fair and public hearing within a reasonable time by an independent and impartial tribunal established by law.

   Judgment shall be pronounced publicly, but the press and public may be excluded from all or part of the trial in the interests of morals, public order or national security in a democratic society where the interests of juveniles or the protection of the private life of the parties so require, or to the extent necessary in the opinion of the court in special circumstances where publicity would prejudice the interests of justice.

2. Everyone charged with a criminal offence shall be presumed innocent until proved guilty according to law.

3. Everyone charged with a criminal offence has the following minimum rights:

   a) to be informed promptly, in a language which he understands and in detail, of the nature and cause of the accusation against him;

   b) to have adequate time and facilities for the preparation of his defence;

   c) to defend himself in person or through legal assistance of his own choosing or, if he has not sufficient means to pay for legal assistance, to be given it free when the interests of justice so require;

   d) to examine or have examined witnesses against him and to obtain the attendance and examination of witnesses on his behalf under the same conditions as witnesses against him;

   e) to have the free assistance of an interpreter if he cannot understand or speak the language used in court.

   These provisions refer to criminal proceedings. However, similar standards are expected for civil proceedings.

☛ When something has to be decided about your rights and responsibilities, you have the right for that decision to be made at a fair and public hearing and within a reasonable time. The hearing must be held before someone who is not involved either with you or with anyone else. It must be a hearing that you can take part in.

The decision at the end of the hearing must be given in public, but the hearing itself may be held in private with only you and the other people involved.

This Article is important for ensuring children's participation in decision-making.

It will usually be clear when the hearing is of a criminal charge.

The question of whether civil rights or obligations are being decided is more difficult. The Strasbourg Court has investigated to see whether the right is private or public in nature. The fact that one of the parties to a dispute is a public body will not decide the matter. If the right at issue has parallels in the private sphere or repercussions on private rights or obligations, it is more likely to be a civil right.

A fair hearing implies that there is:

a) real and effective access to the courts;

b) notice of the time and place of proceedings;

c) a real opportunity to present the case sought to be made (this includes effective participation in proceedings);

d) a reasoned decision.

Paragraph 1 sets out the general principle that everyone is entitled to a fair hearing. This is therefore an important right as regards (a) giving children a hearing at all, and (b) ensuring that the hearing is fair. This is distinct from representation, which merely presents a view of the best interests of children.

Possible issues

The following may give rise to issues under Article 6:

- Hearings that are unfair because they do not cater for the needs of children: for example, dealing with young offenders in adult courts

- Failure to protect the privacy of a child in litigation

- All cases in which a child does not have a voice in determining his or her rights and obligations

- Failure by a public authority to consider and hear all the children affected by its actions

- Failure by schools and local education authorities to hear the child rather than the parent (as criticised by the UN Committee on the Rights of the Child in its 1995 report). This includes exclusion hearings, admissions and special needs.

Cases involving education have so far had little success under the European Convention. In 1989 a dyslexic child, André Simpson, sought a finding that the procedures to determine his special educational needs were in breach of, among others, Article 6. His case failed at the first stage. It was held that Article 6 did not apply to what was an administrative procedure. Since 1989, however, many disputes over statements of special educational needs have been heard by tribunals. The issue might therefore be decided differently today.

Case study

T and V were ten when they killed James Bulger and eleven when they went on trial for his murder. The age of criminal responsibility in England and Wales is ten. Because the offence carried a heavy sentence, the boys were tried in the Crown Court rather than the Youth Court. Unlike proceedings in the Youth Court, those in the Crown Court are public. This trial also had widespread publicity. It was established by the prosecution that the two boys were aware that what they had done was wrong and were therefore responsible under criminal law. They were convicted. On the basis of psychological reports on the boys' perceptions of the trial, the European Court of Human Rights held that although modifications to the Crown Court procedure had been made, the formality and ritual of the court and the publicity that accompanied the trial had meant that the boys were unable to participate effectively in their defence and had not therefore had a fair trial. Following this case, a Practice Direction has now been issued directing courts on how to adapt for children.

See also: *Human Rights Act 1998:* Article 10; Article 14
UN Convention on the Rights of the Child: Article 40

Article 8: The right to respect for private and family life, for home and correspondence

1. Everyone has the right to respect for his private and family life, his home and his correspondence.

2. There shall be no interference by a public authority with the exercise of this right, except such as is in accordance with the law and is necessary in a democratic society in the interests of national security, public safety or the economic well-being of the country, for the prevention of disorder or crime, for the protection of health or morals, or for the protection of the rights and freedoms of others.

☛ **You should not be taken away from your family unless it is for your own good – if, for example, your family is hurting you. Everyone, including your family, should understand that you have things – such as a diary – that you do not want anyone to see.**

This Article is the closest the Act comes to recognising a right to a childhood and to the development of that childhood. It covers the right to an inner life, to the development of relationships with others, to a family life and to a home and correspondence. It covers rights to family life but also to autonomy, whether within or outside the family.

Public authorities must not only not breach these rights but must ensure a right to respect for them. This means that authorities should take steps to enforce respect, whether by refraining from interfering themselves or by ensuring that the rights are not breached in the private sphere.

Private life

The right to have a private life includes issues of personal identity. It also covers bodily integrity.

The right is not limited to having an inner life. It must also comprise the right to establish and develop relationships with other human beings. This will include the right to do so in the social, public sphere. It is no answer to this argument to say that this is a social right, since there is no watertight division between social rights and civil and political rights. This right may in certain circumstances extend to the provision of facilities to give disabled children access to places where they can develop relationships.

For a child in care, state records are "a substitute record for the memories and experience of the child who is not in care". This information is vital to enable a child to understand his or her childhood and early development. It has therefore been held to fall within the scope of private and family life. To make that right effective, the state has a positive obligation to allow access to social services records concerning a child in care, on an application made in adulthood. This principle may be developed in respect of unaccompanied child refugees and information about the whereabouts of family members who are separated from the child as a result of detention, imprisonment, exile, deportation or death. Any conditions imposed on access to such information must be reasonable.

Family life

Whether or not a relationship falls within the scope of family life depends upon the existence of close personal ties. It is arguable that the courts should apply this Article to different types of family, whether they are based on marriage, cohabiting heterosexual partnerships or gay partnerships, or on biological or adoptive or other ties. The Strasbourg Court has left a margin of discretion in deciding which relationships it regards as family ones, although it has recognised the family life of children who are born out of wedlock or who are adopted. UK courts may adopt the approach of the House of Lords in *Fitzpatrick v Stirling Housing Association*, which gave a wide meaning to family life and held that a gay man's long-standing partner was his "family" within the meaning of housing legislation. This will permit children from a variety of backgrounds to claim respect for their family life. Good evidence should be brought of the ties in any particular case.

The mutual enjoyment of each other's company by parent and child is a fundamental element of family life. Only the most pressing grounds can be sufficient to justify the disruption of family ties, and poverty is not such a ground.

However, an abusive parent is unlikely to be able successfully to rely on his or her right to family life over the interests of the child.

Home and correspondence

This is likely to cover interference with the home: for example, by harassment or noise or pollution of the environment. It may also in certain circumstances cover removal or eviction from the home.

Case study

TP and KM were mother and daughter. Over a period of time between 1984 and 1987 the local authority suspected that the child was being sexually abused. A case conference was held, without the mother, and the child was placed on the Child Protection Register. The child, by then aged four, was interviewed by a child psychiatrist. She disclosed that she had been abused; when asked who was responsible, she gave the same first name as that of her mother's boyfriend, but also made other statements that suggested he was not the abuser. The mother was then told that the child had disclosed she had been abused by the boyfriend. A tape of the disclosure interview was not shown to the mother. The local authority was granted a place of safety order and subsequent care and control. The daughter was subsequently rehabilitated. The Commission referred to the principle that mutual enjoyment by the parent and the child of each other's company is a fundamental aspect of family life. It then went on to examine whether the interference with family life fell within the permitted exceptions. It concluded that although the removal of the child as an emergency measure was permitted, the continuance of the measure after the initial stage disclosed a lack of respect for the family life of both mother and child. It also took the view that the mother should have been permitted to view the video of her child's interview as soon as possible. The way the local authority exercised its discretion therefore breached Article 8. The case will now proceed to be heard by the European Court of Human Rights.

Possible issues

The following may give rise to issues under Article 8:

- Removal of children from the family environment by local authorities under the care system

- Decisions of the family courts on contact, residence, adoption and fostering. The rights of the child will need to be considered, as will the rights to family life of any adults involved

- Treatment of children in care

- Separation of children from their families pursuant to decisions under the immigration regime: for example, decisions to deport or to forbid entry

- In the immigration system, the impact of dispersal policies on a child's right to develop within the community

- Separation of children from their families under the criminal justice system. This will arise particularly in decisions on whether to imprison children. Decisions on imprisonment of adults should consider whether the child can have adequate contact with the imprisoned member of their family

- Bullying and freedom from being hurt

- Eviction or removal from the home, or any interference with the enjoyment of an existing home.

See also: *Human Rights Act 1998:* Article 3; Article 6; Article 10; Article 14
UN Convention on the Rights of the Child: Article 9; Article 10; Article 16; Article 20

Article 9: Freedom of religion, thought and conscience

1. Everyone has the right to freedom of thought, conscience and religion; this right includes freedom to change his religion or belief, or freedom, either alone or in community with others and in public or private, to manifest his religion or belief, in worship, teaching, practice and observance.

2. Freedom to manifest one's religion or beliefs shall be subject only to such limitations as are prescribed by law and are necessary in a democratic society in the interests of public safety, for the protection of public order, health or morals, or for the protection of the rights and freedoms of others.

☞ **You have the right openly to follow your own beliefs if this does not interfere with the rights of others.**

Special provision has been made in the Act for the freedom of organised religions. Under Section 13 of the 1998 Act, if a decision by a court (but not by a public authority generally) might affect the exercise by a religious organisation, either collectively or individually, of this freedom, it must have particular regard for this freedom.

This Article may be limited in the ways set out above.

Possible issues

The following may give rise to issues under Article 9:

- The provision of religious or moral education in schools. Pressure to conform to a majority belief may infringe Article 9. The child has a right to follow the belief of his or her parents or family. If, on the other hand, the child is old enough and wishes not to do so, the state should ensure respect for this choice, since the child is not obliged to follow his or her parents' beliefs. Courts have held that the child should not be cut off from exercising his or her options in this matter later on in life

- Provision for religious needs in institutions such as prisons or mental health institutions

- Practices such as male and female genital mutilation may require the state to balance the religion of the parents against the interests and choices of the child.

See also: *UN Convention on the Rights of the Child:* Article 14

Article 10: Freedom of expression and freedom to receive information without interference

1. Everyone has the right to freedom of expression. This right shall include freedom to hold opinions and to receive and impart information and ideas without interference by public authority and regardless of frontiers.

2. The exercise of these freedoms, since it carries with it duties and responsibilities, may be subject to such formalities, conditions, restrictions or penalties as are prescribed by law and are necessary in a democratic society, in the interests of national security, territorial integrity or public safety, for the prevention of disorder or crime, for the protection of health or morals, for the protection of the reputation or rights of others, for preventing the disclosure of information received in confidence, or for maintaining the authority and impartiality of the judiciary.

☛ **You have the right to communicate with other people and say what you think by speaking, writing, making pictures, etc (unless it interferes with the rights of other people). You have the right to collect information from radios, newspapers, television, books, etc, from all over the world. Adults should make sure that you get information you can understand.**

This is an important Article for ensuring that children are able to develop their own voices.

The right to expression is likely to include not only the expression of opinions but also self-development in a wider sense. In the recent cases by gay personnel against the Ministry of Defence, the Strasbourg Court did not rule out that a silence about sexual identity imposed as a result of homophobic policies might constitute an infringement of freedom of expression. In the light of the continued existence in England and Wales of Section 28, it is therefore possible that gay children will be able to rely on this Article.

This Article is also likely to cover dress codes at school, particularly where they affect religious minorities or are based on outdated views of the sexes.

Closely linked to the right to expression is a right to information. Article 10 is not a general freedom of information right, such as would provide a positive right of access to government information. It is essentially a duty not to interfere with the free flow of information, prohibiting the state from restricting a person from receiving information that others may be willing to impart to him.

Case study 1

An organisation in Ireland counselled women – in what was described as a non-directive manner – on available abortion services and related information. It was injuncted from doing so. The organisation brought a complaint that its right to impart information had been breached. It was joined by two individual women who wished to have the information that the organisation was willing to provide.

The Irish Government claimed that its interference with the right to receive and impart information was justified. The organisation relied on statistics showing the damage in human terms resulting from a lack of information. The Court found a breach of Article 10.

Case study 2

D is fifteen years old and has known that he is gay since he was eight. Since attending his secondary school he has received no information about homosexuality, although the sex education course at school has provided a great deal of information about heterosexual sex. He is under the impression that it is criminal to be gay. For this reason, he has revealed to no one that he is attracted to boys. He feels very isolated.

X is a charity set up to provide information about homosexuality. Its request to provide a sex education lesson is refused by D's school.

A religious organisation, which includes parents of children at the school, learns of the request and has a meeting with the school in which it expresses its concern about the possibility that relationships other than marriage are going to be discussed and the lack of moral guidance that this will signal.

This case will raise issues under Article 9 as well as under this Article.

Possible issues

The following may give rise to issues under Article 10:

- Whether a decision adequately allows for the child to express his or her views and to receive information about the decision. This will include inadequate consultation, and the duty will vary with the child's age

- Complaints procedures for children who are users of services

- Age restrictions in respect of school governors, as well as other ways in which children are deprived of a voice in the education system

- The provision of sex education in schools – for example, information about homosexuality or genital mutilation – whether or not the state or the parents wish. Section 28 or local education authority decisions not to provide information may breach a lesbian or gay child's right to information and expression without discrimination, as well as an organisation's right to provide that information

- Interviewing of refugee children, which should be conducted in such a way as to enable them to express themselves

- Children with disabilities should not receive an education that restricts their ability to express themselves or to receive information in a suitable form.

See also: *Human Rights Act 1998:* Article 14

UN Convention on the Rights of the Child: Articles 12 (respect for the views of the child), 13 (freedom of expression) and 17 (access to appropriate information)

Article 11: Freedom of association

1. Everyone has the right to freedom of peaceful assembly and to freedom of association with others, including the right to form and to join trade unions for the protection of his interests.

2. No restrictions shall be placed on the exercise of these rights other than such as are prescribed by law and are necessary in a democratic society in the interests of national security or public safety, for the prevention of disorder or crime, for the protection of health or morals, or for the protection of the rights and freedoms of others. This Article shall not prevent the imposition of lawful restrictions on the exercise of these rights by members of the armed forces, of the police or of the administration of the state.

☛ **You have the right to meet, make friends with and start clubs with other people, unless it interferes with the rights of others.**

Like Articles 9 and 10, this freedom may be restricted.

Even where the aim of a restriction is a legitimate one, such as the imposition of curfews, such restrictions must satisfy the test of being proportionate and necessary. Conditions of detention, whether in the criminal or the immigration sphere, that go beyond what is necessary for a lawful detention may infringe this Article as well as Article 5.

Public order measures aimed at preventing young people from meeting can be challenged under this Article by children as well as by adults.

See also: *Human Rights Act 1998:* Articles 5; Article 8

UN Convention on the Rights of the Child: Article 12; Article 13; Article 14; Article 15; Article 17

Article 14: The right not to be discriminated against in the enjoyment of these rights

The enjoyment of the rights and freedoms set forth in this Convention shall be secured without discrimination on any ground such as sex, race, colour, language, religion, political or other opinion, national or social origin, association with a national minority, property, birth or other status.

☛ **You have these rights whoever you are. If you have special needs and need help to be able to enjoy these rights, help should be given to you.**

Article 14 confers a duty to ensure that rights in the Act are secured without discrimination. It is not a general right to equality. If the inequality does not fall within the scope of at least one other right, this Article cannot be relied on.

The approach of the Strasbourg Court has been to regard it as unnecessary to look at this right if a breach of one of the other rights has been found. If, however, there is inequality in the enjoyment of the right that falls short of a breach, this right becomes more important: for example, if a child seeking asylum does not enjoy the same full Article 8 rights as other children.

This Article applies to children as well as to adults.

As well as being protected in their own right, children will be protected if they are discriminated against as a result of the status of their parents: for example, if the children of prisoners suffer an interference with their right to family life.

"Other status" covers all grounds not specifically mentioned, such as sexuality, age, disability, being a Traveller or being an asylum-seeker. Age discrimination covers discrimination between children of different ages and between children and adults.

The non-discrimination covers:

• Differential treatment where there should be equal treatment

• Failure to accommodate special needs so as to ensure equality or enjoyment of a right, since to treat different matters equally in a mechanical way would be as unjust as to treat equal matters differently.

This Article covers the right to be equal in law (forbidding, for example, differential ages of consent) but also covers equality in fact: for example, the denial in practice of an education to Traveller children.

The Article also covers discrimination between children and adults. As explained above, this covers not only arbitrary distinctions between children and adults, but also situations where children are unable to enjoy a right because of a failure to address a special need.

Possible issues

The following may give rise to issues under Article 14:

- Assumptions that children are automatically disqualified from participating in decisions about their healthcare

- Differential ages of consent

- Differential treatment of refugee children

- Discrimination against Travelling children in the education system

- Failures in systems to accommodate the special needs of children

- Unequal protection against assault.

See also: every other Article.
UN Convention on the Rights of the Child: Article 2

Protocol 1, Article 2: Education

No person shall be denied the right to education. In the exercise of any functions which it assumes in relation to education and to teaching, the state shall respect the right of parents to ensure such education and teaching is in conformity with their own religious and philosophical convictions.

☞ **You have the right to go to school. If your parents and your school do not agree about what you should learn, the school should listen to what your parents want, unless that would be bad for you.**

The UK reserved to itself, when signing the UN Convention on the Rights of the Child, the power not to provide this right if it conflicts with the efficient provision of education to others or involves unreasonable public expenditure. This reservation remains in the Human Rights Act 1998, although it may be open to challenge.

Note that the right in the first part of this Article is the child's, while that in the second part is the parents'. It is a striking feature of education law in England that the rights of children, in contrast to those of parents, are rarely recognised.

In draft, the first part of this Article read "Everyone has the right to an education", but this was later changed to the present negative wording. The new version appears to require the state only to leave children the freedom to be educated, rather than to ensure that they are educated. The European Court of Human Rights has held, in the context of a claim brought by a linguistic minority, that this does not require a state to subsidise private education or to create a certain type of education. However, the Court rejected the argument on behalf of the Belgian Government that the right was merely a freedom to be educated. It pointed out that the right had to be effective: that is to say, it had to be a real rather than a paper right. This included a right of access to the education that was in existence at the time.

In the same case, the Court went on to hold that the right to education is a right whose extent is to be defined in the light of each country's social and economic development. In the country in question, Belgium, the right meant education to higher level.

The second part of the Article recognises the rights of parents who may hold minority convictions. Where education or funding for education is provided to the children of parents with more mainstream opinions, there may be a breach of the right not to be discriminated against in the enjoyment of this right. The state may seek to rely on the cost of providing this education. Indeed, cases brought by parents of disabled children segregated within the education system have failed on this ground. Few of the cases involved complaints by the children themselves.

In the case of children from minority communities, the parental right may clash with the child's view on whether they want to be educated in line with their parent's convictions. It is likely that, unless not to do so would foreclose the child's options later in life, affect the child's health and safety or amount to a breach of another right, the state would not intervene.

In education law, a child is defined as someone under eighteen. There is little consultation of children in the education system or recognition of them as persons: for example, no governor of an educational system (except further education institutions) may be under eighteen. There is no provision for children to be parties to exclusion or special needs hearings.

Checklist

Are children given a voice at school?

Are children given a voice in exclusion or other disciplinary procedures?

Are all children provided with adequate information, including sex education?

Are there clear standards for separate schools? Do these take into account cultural differences?

Possible issues

The following may give rise to issues under Protocol 1, Article 2:

- The effect of dispersal on refugee children, if movement around the country prevents them from obtaining an effective education

- The segregation of children with special educational needs or disabilities as well as inadequate provision of education for them

- The failure to provide an education that reflects minority traditions, particularly for children from those traditions

- How far a local education authority acts effectively to enforce attendance at school

- The adequacy of education in care, mental health, detention or other institutions

- The adequacy of exclusion procedures and the education given to excluded children

- Bullying

- Provision of sex education

- Class sizes

- Imbalances between secular and religious schools.

See also: *Human Rights Act 1998:* Article 3; Article 6; Article 8; Article 9; Article 10; Article 14
UN Convention on the Rights of the Child: Article 28; Article 14; Article 29(1)

Action checklist

Has there been an act or omission that is incompatible with any of the rights, or with equal enjoyment of the rights, set out in this booklet?

Is there permissible interference with the right?

Consider this point carefully and seek advice if in doubt. If the answer is No, proceed.

Is the breach the direct and only possible result of statute?

If Yes, seek a declaration of incompatibility. Only certain courts can do this, and you should take further advice.

Has the right been breached by a public authority or a body exercising a public function?

If Yes, identify it.

If No, is a public authority otherwise closely involved?

If No, remember the obligation of the courts.

Is there a person or persons who run(s) a risk of being a victim of an act or omission which is incompatible with the rights set out in the Act?

Are they under eighteen?

Are they able to act for themselves?

If No, consider who should act as their litigation friend. Certain procedures must be followed by those who act as a litigation friend, and further advice should be sought.

Is there an organisation that either can act as litigation friend or is itself a victim?

Does the issue arise in legal proceedings?

If No, consider negotiating with the public authority before starting legal proceedings.

Consider the relevant time limits.

Seek legal advice if in doubt.

Does the issue arise as a defence in proceedings brought by a public authority: for example, in possession proceedings or a prosecution? If Yes, it can be raised at any time.

Does it arise within the context of other proceedings? If Yes, the time limits applicable to those proceedings apply.

Does it arise as a free-standing claim under the Human Rights Act? If Yes, the Act says it must be raised within one year of the act or omission. The Act makes no provision for time to run only from when a child reaches eighteen, unlike parallel legislation for general claims in civil law. This may give rise to issues in respect of access to courts on the basis of genuine equality. However, the cautious approach will be to treat the one-year time limit as applying to children. This will also have the advantage of litigating the claim while it is fresh. A court may also hear a claim within such a longer period as is fair to all, and this should be used where there is a delay between the act or omission and the child's or relatives' seeking assistance.

Ms Stubbings and others brought legal action in respect of sexual abuse as children. Ms Stubbings did not realise the link between her mental health problems and the abuse until she was thirty-two years old – fifteen years after the abuse.

Where an act is a breach of duty, time limits start to run from the date of knowledge. There is also a discretion to allow a claim as of right despite its being out of time. However, the House of Lords held that sexual abuse is an intentional act which is not a breach of duty. Time therefore ran from the age of eighteen for six years.

On an application to the European Court, the court held that there was no breach of Article 6, since the restriction placed by limitation rules was within the margin of appreciation. The court appeared to place some weight on the fact that time ran from eighteen. However, it did also say that the court "must be satisfied that the limitations applied do not restrict or reduce the access left to the individual in such a way or to such an extent that the very essence of the right is impaired". The Court went on to refer to the possibility of enacting specific provisions in cases of child abuse.

What do you want to achieve by raising the issue?

- To seek an interpretation of the law that is compatible with the Act
- To seek a declaration of incompatibility
- A change in the law
- A change in a decision or in a practice in a particular case or generally to seek a finding that there has been a breach
- To seek a declaration of practice that is compatible with the Act
- Compensation for a person (a court can award this, taking into account the level of awards before the Strasbourg court)
- Recovery of costs in pursuing the claim.

Useful contacts

For information on children's rights:

www.savethechildren.org.uk
Save the Children
Save the Children Public Enquiry Unit tel 020 7703 5400

www.crin.org
Child Rights Information Network
Run by Save the Children; contains index of other organisations

eurochild.gla.ac.uk
Centre for Europe's Children
Documentation centre set up by the Council of Europe and UNICEF

www.echr.coe.int
European Court of Human Rights
Full search of case law available

www.beagle.org.uk/hra
Case law of the ECHR

www.unicef
UNICEF

For official publications:

www.cabinet-office.gov.uk (seu/1990)

www.publications.parliament.uk

For further information and support:

Childline (tel 0800 1111)

Childline HQ (tel 020 7239 1000)

Children's Rights Commissioner/Ministers for Children in Wales and Scotland

Children's Rights Office (tel 020 7278 8222, e-mail crights@ftech.co.uk)

Children's Legal Centre (helpline tel 01206 873820, e-mail www2.essex.ac.uk/c&acu)

Community Legal Service (www.justask.org.uk)

Office of Children's Rights Commissioner for London (tel 020 7278 4390,
e-mail **team@londonchildrenscommissioner.org.uk**,
www.londonchildrenscommissioner.org.uuk)

Children's Rights Commissioner for Oxfordshire (tel 01865 792 662)

Children's Rights Officers and Advocates (CROA) (tel 020 8748 7413
mail@croa1.freeserve.co.uk)

Children's Rights Catalogues detailing publications and resources are available from
SC UK Publication Sales
Save the Children
17 Grove Lane
London SE5 8RD
020 7703 5400
e-mail **publications@scfuk.org.uk**

Glossary of key terms

clawback clauses   Clauses that allow a state to interfere with a right.

derogation   The state cannot under any circumstances go back on its duty under Articles 2, 3, 4(1) and 7. These are "non-derogable". It can, however, "derogate from" or suspend the rights under the other Articles in time of war or public emergency, provided the measures it takes do not go beyond what is strictly necessary and do not amount to a breach of other international law obligations.

margin of appreciation   The Strasbourg Court recognised that it was a court which was removed from local societies and that national authorities were in a better position to make some judgements about human rights. This included, for example, matters of morality and other matters which might vary from state to state. There is disagreement about whether this margin will apply to national courts which are closer to society.

positive obligation   A duty to do something, in contrast to a duty not to do something but merely to permit a freedom without interference.

progressive rights   Rights that will vary in their extent according to the social and economic development of the country.

proportionality   This is a key principle in considering clawback clauses. A proper balance of rights must be struck between the interests of the individual and the interests of society in general. This means that even where the interference is in the name of a permitted aim, it will still be unlawful if it goes beyond what is necessary to achieve that aim. This may be because there are measures are available, or because the essence of the right is destroyed or because the means are out of all proportion to the end.

Protocol   A protocol is an addition to a Convention, agreed after the main body of the Convention. Once it is agreed by enough states, it has the same status as the Convention.

Issue-based index

Asylum-seekers, see refugee children

Care, children in, or otherwise outside their family
- care records: Art 8
- failure to protect from abuse and neglect: Art 3
- wrongful, including excessively lengthy, removal from the family: Art 8
- detention: Art 5

Child soldiers: Art 4

Court, children in
- defendants, witnesses: Art 6

Disabilities, children with
- consider under all other categories
- segregation in school: Protocol 1, Art 2; Art 3; Art 14
- inadequate consultation and information: Art 10
- conditions in care or detention: Art 3
- medical treatment: Art 2; Art 3

Family, children within
- definition of family: Art 8
- separation from family: Art 8
- abuse, neglect or beating by family: Art 3
- conflict with parents on decisions, eg, medical: Art 10; Art 6
- children discriminated against because of their family: Art 14

Housing: Art 3; Art 8

Mental health
- detention: Art 5
- conditions in detention: Art 3; Art 5
- discrimination: Art 14

Migrants
- effect of dispersal: Art 8
- deportation of: Art 2, Art 3
- detention: Art 3, Art 5
- education, Protocol 1, Art 2

Prisoners' children
- right to family life: Art 8
- conditions in detention: Art 3

Refugee children
- consider under all other categories
- education: Protocol 1, Art 2
- unaccompanied and accompanied children: Art 8
- interviewing children: Art 10
- effect of dispersal: Art 8
- deportation: Art 2; Art 3
- detention: Art 3; Art 5

School, children at
- bullying: Art 3
- special educational needs: Art 3; Protocol 1
- exclusion: Protocol 1
- sex, sexuality, race, disability or other discrimination: Art 3
- segregation of disabled children: Art 3; Protocol 1, Art 2